Even in my dreams

For Hatchi

(Where would we be without you?)

&

The little lambs that inspired this book

EVEN IN MY DREAMS

A collection of vegan poems

Edited by Emma Letessier

Many thanks to Linda Monahan, whose poem provided the title for this collection. Thanks also to Honey Morris for her love and support. All profits from the sale of this book go towards the Barefoot Vegan Farm & Animal Sanctuary - www.barefootveganfarm.com

EVEN IN MY DREAMS. First published in 2016.

No part of this publication may be used or reproduced without the written permission of the author/s.

© 2016 Emma Letessier (selection and introduction)

The acknowledgment of contributors on page 134 constitutes an extension of this copyright notice.

ISBN 978-1-326-77441-7

Design by Emma Letessier

Cover image & illustration on page 3 used with permission from www.freepix.com

Animal illustrations by Tropinina Olga, shutterstock.com.

Typeset by Emma Letessier

CONTENTS

Introduction — *Emma Letessier*   11

Vegan takes time — *Anthony Rhead*   14
Let them live — *Philip Kiernan*   15
To recognise our bond — *Alizée Ventderrmidi*   18
Change is good — *Kat von Cupcake*   19
Heaven — *Philip McCulloch-Downs*   21
Earth cries — *Sky Raven the Vegan Poet*   23
What would aliens say? — *Damien Clarkson*   26
Animal mineral miserable — *Marc McGowan*   27
Keepers of our souls — *Gunjan Bhatia*   30
Even in my dreams — *Linda Monahan*   34
Up on the hill — *Emma Letessier*   35
A vegan life — *Anthony Rhead*   37
We live in the city — *Alizée Ventderrmidi*   39
Those little deaths — *Ashley Capps*   40
Blood or blood — *Robbie Nuwanda*   41
Backwards — *Emma Letessier*   43
I keep the animals in my heart — *Atara Schimmel*   44
5 4 3 2 one — *Gabriel Colnic*   45
The story of a mother and child — *Emily Atkinson-Dalton*   46

Calf — *Nathan Hicks*　48
The igloo calf — *Rekha Padinjattakathu*　49
Caged — *Karl Drinkwater*　51
Time — *Nicola McLean*　52
If only… — *Susan Buckland*　53
Percy — *Nicola Alexandra Evans*　54
Coventry — *Karl Drinkwater*　55
Please sir — *Nicola McLean*　56
The beast — *Mango Wodzak*　57
Empathy enzyme — *Robbie Nuwanda*　60
What became of you, my beloved? — *Emma Letessier*　63
Catch of the day — *Nancy Correa*　65
Devil's shores — *Lenny Marignier*　66
Thresher — *Susan Richardson*　67
Fetch — *Susan Richardson*　68
Springtime — *Philip McCulloch-Downs*　69
My friend, my girl, my Glenda — *Honey Morris*　72
Sarah undefeated — *Nancy Correa*　74
Goat power — *Kat von Cupcake*　75
I used to be a zombie — *Mango Wodzak*　76
I don't care — *Philip McCulloch-Downs*　78
The hunter — *Emma Letessier*　80
The dog is running madly round the office — *Karl Drinkwater*　83
If animals spoke English — *Mango Wodzak*　84
No joyrides — *Kat von Cupcake*　87

A vegan from Slough — *Dominic Berry*   88
The vegan troll — *Emma Letessier*   89
Silly me — *Philip McCulloch-Downs*   90
Peaches — *Mango Wodzak*   91
Mary had a little lamb — *Mango Wodzak*   92
Nutty — *Cathy Bryant*   93
Comfort food — *Linda Monahan*   95
The myth of protein — *Dominic Berry*   96
Vegan is the food of love — *Cathy Bryant*   98
Ingredients — *Charles Waters*   99
The vegan macho nacho secret — *Marc McGowan*   100
Fruit not flesh — *Mango Wodzak*   102
A gay vegan limerick — *Dominic Berry*   104
Earth angels — *Atara Schimmel*   105
Wolfen me — *Nancy Correa*   106
Awake Part I — *Gunjan Bhatia*   107
Awake Part II — *Gunjan Bhatia*   109
Awake Part III — *Gunjan Bhatia*   111
For white vegans who claim the flesh of others — *Sea Sharp*   113
Kindly — *Ashley Capps*   115
Nature — *Mango Wodzak*   120
We will — *M. "Butterflies" Katz*   122
I will take you to the sunshine — *Atara Schimmel*   124
Wolf moon — *Nancy Correa*   126
My pledge — *Keith Lupton*   127

Homecoming — *Gunjan Bhatia* 128
Heart overhead — *Robin Raven* 129
For the freedom and peace of all beings on Earth — *Linda Monahan* 131
Vegan pagan prayer — *Dianne Sylvan* 133

Poem Contributors — 134

INTRODUCTION

Why a book of vegan poetry? To be quite honest, it wasn't something I had intended to do but nonetheless, after reading the submissions from other vegan poets, I now believe it to have been divinely inspired. The idea came to me one morning while I was walking our dog, Hatchi, up near the chateau in the village where we used to live in the East of France.

It was springtime and I took great pleasure in watching the lambs bounding with such *joie de vivre*. However, as always when you view things through the lens of veganism, my pleasure was tinged with sadness as I considered the fate that lay in store for these babies and the grief the mothers would soon experience in having their children taken from them.

Contemplating this scene, lines of poetry filled my head – this became the poem I entitled *Backwards* (page 43) – along with the idea that I had to try and put together a book of vegan poetry. I hadn't written any poetry since my university days.

Writing poetry with a vegan theme has become a cathartic exercise for me, a healthy way to cope with the existential angst I sometimes feel gurgling around inside of me. I'm sure the other poets in this anthology would agree.

For vegans, poetry allows us to take emotions that are raw and painful and transform them into something beautiful, powerful. A metamorphosis takes place where the images of oppression that we have borne witness to, emerge cleansed and renewed through the written word.

As the reader, the poems in this book allow you to explore the full spectrum of emotions we all experience as vegans. There are poems that speak with joy, sadness, despair, horror, frustration, confusion, triumph, hope, gratitude, humour and sarcasm.

What will vegans get from this book? I hope you'll feel inspired and strangely comforted by the confirmation that the feelings you experience as a vegan are not unique, you are not alone. Maybe you'll find yourself drawn to put pen to paper, encouraged to create art as a vehicle for beautiful activism.

And for the non-vegans, you are offered a vital glimpse of the world through our eyes, a chance to lift the veil, allow yourself to feel our compassion for the suffering of other sentient beings and understand the very tangible consequences of our everyday choices.

I would like to also make a special note about Sea Sharp's poem: *For white vegans who claim the flesh of others* (page 113). If you're a white vegan, how do you feel when you read Sea's words? Challenged? Offended? That's a good place to start and I would encourage you to keep digging deeper with an open heart and an open mind. When promoting veganism, it's important that we are conscious of how our words and actions impact on others. When we animalise the bodies of others and the oppressor is absent from our 'viral memes' comparing the suffering of animals to the slavery of other humans, we disempower and. alienate entire populations of people. We dismiss other forms of oppression such as racism, sexism, and ableism. If someone is telling us that what we're doing is hurting them, we have a responsibility to stop, listen and understand their point-of-view and then decide how we can change our actions. Only by doing so, will we be an inclusive and diverse movement, working together to try to alleviate the suffering of all. Intersectional veganism offers us the opportunity to shine a light on the links that connect all forms of oppression. If I were to put together another anthology of vegan poetry, I would seek to include more works of an intersectional nature.

Finally, I want to thank all the contributors who have donated their poems. I am so honoured that you wanted to be part of this project. And I also want to thank you, reader, for purchasing this book.

You have made a contribution toward the founding and maintaining of the Barefoot Vegan Farm & Animal Sanctuary, my dream and life purpose intertwined. You have my immense gratitude.

Emma Letessier, 2016

VEGAN TAKES TIME

Vegan takes time
Its conscience is deep
A growth that's divine
Once you've taken that leap…

Anthony Rhead

LET THEM LIVE

There once lived an evil monster
Taller and bigger than we are
In every being across the land
He instilled incalculable fear

"To repeatedly make us pregnant
He'd forcefully inseminate us
And upon our beloved babies born
He'd cruelly separate us"

He mercilessly stole the offspring
And took the milk they craved
Cracking precious maternal bonds
For a thirst perverse and depraved

"He carved off our beaks and caged us"
"He smoked our hives and enraged us"
"He cut off our wool and froze us"
"It's true. Ask anyone who knows us"

Captive, hopeless, frightened, doomed
All so their flesh could be consumed
He called it beef and named it bacon
But it was the bodies he had taken

Eggs - yes eggs - were even plundered
Those perfect pods of potential
Hens distraught at having been caught
Never to see chicks emerging

You may be thinking that's bad enough
but sadly it's far from all
There was another awful atrocity
That's sure to make your skin crawl

Countless crying victims dragged
And destroyed without a care
In putrid houses filled with slaughter
To extract their outer layer

Skin from a murdered innocent
Such a gruesome monstrosity
Euphemistically labelled leather
And presented as luxury

An incurable compulsion for slaying
An insatiable appetite for pain
Capture, keep, kill, repeat
No one escaped during his reign

Bolts through the brain
He claimed it humane
They believed him

Slice through the throat
So quick they don't know it
They believed him

But killing one who wishes to be
It's the antithesis of humanity
It's a crime against creation
Believing differently is insanity

They want to survive
They want to think
They want to breathe
They want to blink
And sometimes gaze
and sneeze and laze
and, like you, live.
Will you let them?

Philip Kiernan

TO RECOGNIZE OUR BOND

I am a cat.
I am a pig, a chicken, a cow.
I am a dog.
I am a rabbit, a goose, a sheep.

Today,
You take my life.
Yesterday,
You buried love.

I am a baby.
I am old, tired, ill.
I am a friend.
I am forgotten, lost, alone.

Today,
You learn to love equally,
Tomorrow,
We can live together.

Alizée Ventderrmidi

CHANGE IS GOOD

The sky is blue,
but not my mood.
I was rescued today,
and will not be your food.

No more days at the factory,
those machines were so scary.
Humans are so silly,
there is no reason for dairy.

There are soy beans and nuts,
and plants from the ground
that make yummy milk and cheeses;
such choices abound.

It makes such good sense
and it's easy to see,
you should eat what I eat,
instead of eating me.

Kat von Cupcake

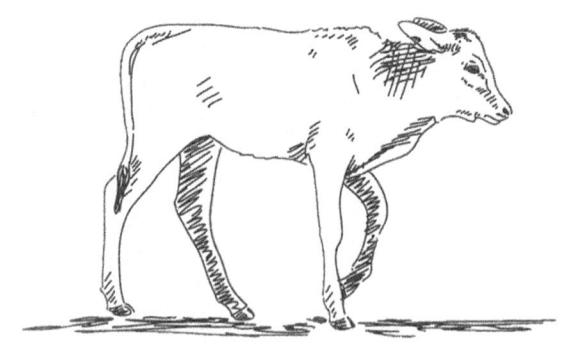

HEAVEN

Ahh, look at them in the fields
All happy and smiling and free
(Well, I *think* that they are smiling
It's tricky for me to see
As this barbed wire round the fence
Keeps them at a distance)
But I guess it must be really
A *jolly* nice existence!
I wouldn't mind that life -
Roaming in the grass
(Although, on second thoughts, the ground
Looks a little sparse…)
But what *bliss* beneath the sun
With the greenery and flowers
And regulation food dispensed
At regulation hours
By hands that hold them safely and
Comfort and protect them and
Take their teeth and tails and
Brand them and inject them
Their bodies, pink and white and brown
Grow big and fat and healthy
And their babies are removed
So their owners can stay wealthy
It must be *wonderful* to have
No worries in your head
No cares or understanding
That soon you will be dead

Ahh, bless the cute and cuddly ones
That decorate our land
But - let them all die kicking
By someone *else's* hand
Please spare me the sight of their
Piss and shit and fear
As the sharp and bloody cutting blade
Efficiently draws near
And they're drained and sliced and minced
And forced into my belly
Skinned for cheap and nasty shoes
And rendered into jelly

But

Let's keep that under wraps
Don't spoil the lovely lie
That *all* God's little creatures
Go to heaven when they die

Philip McCulloch-Downs

EARTH CRIES

Every time that I close my eyes I can hear the Earth cry…

And I sigh,
because I know I try,
to make this place better.
I watch my people die,
they don't listen with their heart;
they try to fight me with their mind,
they're really fighting with themselves,
a truth I hope that they can find. Enlightenment,
is seeing yourself in all elements,
all elements in you,
A universal truth,
that binds all of our mother's youth.

Every time that I close my eyes I can hear the Earth cry…

When a creature goes extinct,
we lose a piece of ourselves;
depleting the oceans and ozone,
creating a hell,
which has no fury like a woman's wrath.
If she sheds tears for too long,
they turn into a warpath.
Blood baths at the slaughterhouse,
deplete the water while you're screaming, "Drought!"

I'm standing there confused like,
"What you talkin bout?
You're wasting water on the animals,
you plan to eat.
One burger is two months of showers,
Try to understand that, please."

Because every time that I close my eyes I can hear the Earth cry…

I see her in me and me in her.
She flows through my bloodstream,
like the rivers of birth.
She is the giver of life,
and we abuse what's hers,
for the taste of rotting flesh.
They've mastered the taste of death,
and now it's so profitable,
it's an industrial complex,
in an industry sustained,
by the destruction of what's left.
The truth never sells,
but they sell destruction well,
that's truth, it never fails.
Flesh makes your body stale,
yet we obsess on killing innocents,
in a system of imprisonment.
Where there's a war on blacks,
like the Nazi's attacked the Jews;
but it's far worse for animals,
literally treated as food.

Yes, every time that I close my eyes I can hear the Earth cry…

It doesn't even matter,
how we got so confused.
What matters is how to change it,
when our minds are so abused.
I listen to her cries,
and share her emotions with you,
and hope that when you close your eyes you can hear them too.
Her sadness is apparent,
but it's changing real fast.
Fresh water's turning blood red,
our destruction will be vast,
and history will record,
all of the questions we didn't ask.
Like, "Was the taste of meat worth,
all of the methane gas,
or the water that we wasted,
right down to the last?"

Every time I close my eyes I can hear the earth cry
and sometimes so do I

Sky Raven the Vegan Poet

WHAT WOULD ALIENS SAY?

What would they say, if aliens landed here today?

I think they would dismay.

At all the war, the pain and hate.

Our planet was green.

Until we made it less serene.

Our oceans were clean.

But oil, plastic and chemicals left their stain.

I'd probably go back.

Rather than watch this world's heart attack.

It's like we are on crack.

And greed has us never going back.

Damien Clarkson

ANIMAL VEGETABLE MISERABLE

Animal + vegetable = miserable
A vegan thinks
Animals for food is criminal
And that stinks

Can't we eat food
The grows on trees?
Why not have meals
From Fruits and beans?

It's not too hard
To change our thoughts
Away from killing
And more feed lots

No more suffering
No more sickness
It starts with the animal
But the truth is this...

These behaviors affect us
And change who we are
Would you eat a pig
You hit with your car?

So sort out your thoughts
About life and death
You will soon realize
You're not right in the head

If you keep eating meat
It's just not sustainable
You have to make a change
To what's on your table

If we don't change
This killing culture
We are no better
Than people who torture

So let's love animals
And let them live free
Let's stop the killing
Of you and of me

Let's truly believe
That life is all sacred
Instead of some justification
Of the animals imprisoned and bred

Maybe if we love
Just a little bit more
We will realize
What life is for

To find freedom
 And happiness
To live full
And hear this

If we can eat each meal
And somehow nothing dies
We will have found the secret
To living compassionate lives

Marc McGowan

KEEPERS OF OUR SOULS

They exist as fragments
Tethered to our broken core
Controlled by the chains of our will
they walk beside us
As though our soul decided to leave our body
in hope of escape
but couldn't get far enough.

They exist as fragments
behind illustrated smiles
on screens and shelves
that mask their suffering
and reduce their existence
to objects of consumption.
As if consuming their tattered hearts
would mend our own.

They exist as fragments
Their power reduced to heads above mantles
and iron emblems on hoods of cars.
Our claim to power in this world -
The frozen roars of stolen spirits
The frozen freedom of captive souls

They exist as fragments
In memories of lost companions
reflected in somber eyes behind bars
that reach out in vain,
to touch the innocence of laughing children.
In bodies that rest against glass walls
knowing that freedom lies on the other side
just inches away
but out of reach.

Empty souls in captive bodies
created by us
in our quest to conserve
what was only meant to be free.

They exist as fragments
In "a life well lived"
A life enslaved,
where freedom exists
but only as words on the sides of a box.
Humanely raised
as means to an end.
A false existence
well aligned with our own pretensions
To hide the wounds we bear
and inflict.

They exist as fragments
In the innocent eyes of gentle souls
who fall asleep in their arms each night.
Of little hands that grasp with love
the soft bodies of their favorite friends.
Little words and little thoughts
that learn about our world, first through theirs.
Voices that delight in familiar sounds,
the Baa-s and Moo-s of childhood
soon appear cut and drowned in sauces
or whipped over cakes
to mark the end of innocence.
A friendship forgotten and forever changed
by the voices of our own broken years.

They exist as fragments

They are the keepers of our souls
The silent guardians of our world
pushed to the fringes
in our quest to complete our broken selves.

We exist as fragments

As ghosts of our own making
waiting to be noticed
and returned
to freedom.

Gunjan Bhatia

EVEN IN MY DREAMS

The soft soil of my beloved
Earth was cluttered with bones
and cracked hooves. Orphaned
calves cried me to sleep.

The waters freely given, clean
and steady falling, washed
blood from abattoir floors,
tainted and misused.

The feathered breeze, uplifting
leaves, wings, hearts,
choked chickens, billions,
in ammonia-clogged warehouses.

I am awake after one too many
nightmares. My eyes will never
close again: even in my dreams
I am vegan.

I heard once that to dream in another
tongue is the mark of true fluency.
The new language is then second
nature, a part of you, and I say again:

Even in my dreams I am vegan.

Linda Monahan

UP ON THE HILL

You and I
We sit together under the shade of a tree.
You lay your body across my feet
Close your eyes as I stroke your belly.
There is an understanding
A closeness
Love.
I feel your sensibility
Your fear, your joy, your pain.

Science says…
"Don't try and anthropomorphise these beasts!"
But science can't explain everything
It's always reassessing and reinterpreting what is "true"
And most people fear what they don't understand.

When I open my mind and listen to my heart
I don't need someone qualified, white-coated, stuffy and official
To tell me the whisperings of my soul…
Or to try and build a wall around my heart
Creating conditioned compartments
Where I can file each being based on their scientific validations

"We are the same, but we are different"
My heart beats out this reminder
As I gaze out upon the cows in the field
Who communicate and interact together in ways I don't yet understand

While I try not to reflect upon the grizzly fate they will meet
Once their *organic, free-range, humane* life is spent.

It is easy and difficult to forget the sufferings of the world
When it's just you and me sitting together quietly.

Emma Letessier

A VEGAN LIFE

It gave to me
the greatest gift
a newfound health
from just one shift

A vegan life
Has changed my days
I see the world
In clearer ways

I see the cruel
And desperate plights
For sentient beings
With life and rights

I see a world where
Greed is good
To take a life
To spill their blood

I don't believe
I like these ways
I like a life
Where nature stays

Yet still we take
We steal and rob
We justify
for we need that job

This golden land
May one day fall
We take too much
Of what's meant for all.

Anthony Rhead

WE LIVE IN THE CITY

Still have some vegan pizza,
there's no sunset downtown.
I know you won't be home.

A stray cat and I found each other,
we followed the moon between the buildings.
I used to be scared at night remember?

I can hear the TV from my garden,
a balcony for bell peppers and sleepy cats.
I have always wanted a sunny temple.

Alizée Ventderrmidi

THOSE LITTLE DEATHS

White toads on the road
so small we didn't even feel them
flatten beneath our shoes.
And mosquitos – nebulous
clouds we'd clap out, summer
evening's porch talk punctuated,
always by that strange applause.
Orb-weavers descended at dusk
From their daytime roosts –warm
leaves, the husks of magnolias –
and fastened their threadbare laundry
through the trees. I remember
an enormous spider we smashed,
the difficult flag she's put up
in our doorframe, the way
she just hung in the middle
and breathed. How soon
we dropped our sticks and turned
to our mother's night-blooming
moonflower; how we cherished
the frantic star it made
against the growing dark.

Ashley Capps

BLOOD OR BLOOD

When your family are immoral,
Where does your loyalty lie?
Is it with the blood that's yours,
Or that's spilt and left to dry?

For indeed the crimson cries,
Are multiples of what's my own.
Then ponder so my stance,
To condemn rather than condone.

For the guilty have no defence,
But that they do not care.
To dare to call such horror evil,
Is deemed to be unfair.

For in a family the crime
Is worse to tell the truth.
Than that which takes the lives of many,
To challenge, this seems uncouth.

Personal choice has no place,
When the victim has not theirs.
A life is here involved and taken,
Not just choosing to wear flares.

My morals are not subjective,
I cannot miss people out.
For my view on right and wrong,
Never suffers from such a drought.

For family there is no room,
To seat yourself on the fence.
My loyalty lies in the wake,
With not guilt but innocence.

Robbie Nuwanda

BACKWARDS

Although I seek to do no harm
and keep an open heart
You turn away from me with repulsion.
But if by some unhappy forgetting
I were to find myself again
glistening knife in hand
to cut the throat of the lamb
(In this world that lusts for its own destruction)
You would welcome me with open arms
and together we would blindly bathe in blood.

Emma Letessier

I KEEP THE ANIMALS IN MY HEART

I keep the animals in my heart at all times.
Though they are far away, locked behind bars, caged and confined in dark and tortured warehouses,
I feel them here with me, inside my heart, at all times.
Though I cannot hear their cries and pleas for help with my ears,
I can hear their cries and pleas for help with my heart.
I vow to keep you in my heart at all times.
I vow to bring your plight, your suffering, and your beauty into the light.
I vow to share my love of you with everyone that touches my life.

Atara Schimmel

5 4 3 2 one

Five reasons to love you, no reasons to hate

Four things to tell you, before it's too late

Three minutes left, before I disappear

Two seconds alone, just with you my dear

One last time, before I say adieu, my dear baby

I love y…

Gabriel Colnic

THE STORY OF A MOTHER AND CHILD

When I was a young child,
A little girl came to me.
Curious and inquisitive,
The last in a row of three.

The young girl reached out her hand,
Her mother by her side,
And as I suckled upon her fingers,
The little girl asked "Why?"

Mother looked down at innocent eyes,
And said in tone sincere
"She cannot suckle upon her mother
To drink her milk, my dear."

The girl looked down at my weary head
and then across to the other
Pen that stood across the room
For there was my mother.

I saw her eyes glance at me
As she stood in her pen,
Her sore udders had just been milked
And she was pregnant again.

The girl gave me a final pat
With pity in her eyes
I didn't blame her for believing
The comforting white lies.

"I'm sorry for what I've done"
She said, "I didn't know back then
I will no longer separate mother and daughter
I will never drink milk again."

Emily Atkinson-Dalton

CALF

Haphazardly creating;
Artists of madness
Careful at first
Soon reckless and wild.

My brothers and sisters
Birthed like sketches
Quick and light-hearted
For now.

Cages so tight
Bound like Moleskine
Never to know
Never to learn.

Air holes above me
Light floods the scene
The only kindness
Shines on your creation.

Gnarled and sinewy
Awkward and unamused
I stumble out
And you erase me.

Nathan Hicks

THE IGLOO CALF

Long dark lashes, deep brown eyes
Creamy-white coat with a tinge of beige
Tender ears pierced by numbered tags,
There he stands, barely a week into life!

Seeking the love of a mother
He was not allowed to suckle;
In every stroking finger that is alas,
Stained by grief or by guilt!

His innocence sears my heart
For now, I too am party to the crime
By the mere knowledge of the grim fate
That he so naively awaits!

I try to wash my conscience clear,
With the fact that I haven't touched meat
In decades; And never will;
Still, his mellow gaze hounds me home,
Oh! That guileless form weighs my soul!

As long as wilful ignorance reigns
In what fills the world platter,
Into the misery of solitary confinement
Are born, more and more igloo calves!

If, as the wise man opines,
Compassion is indeed a verb;
Being Vegan
Seems the sole humane recourse,
The only conscious path!

Rekha Padinjattakathu

CAGED

It thrashed in panic, desperate for escape;
But dull ache became jabbing agony,
Ebbing only after it mewled in pain;
Stopped moving; gave in. Its raw legs were trapped.

A stench like loosened bowels and acrid smoke,
Sharp throbbing from the legs upwards, hot head.
Voices assured her she would be okay,
But no escape from the scream of torn flesh.

Lights shone in her stinging eyes and she blinked:
Stickiness, something had run into them.
Looking down (the only painless movement):
A dark, wet stain on her going-out dress …

… *New Year's Eve.*

She'd been keen to get home, it was so cold.
They started to cut her out with grinders.
Red sparks flashing she turned, saw Tom, and screamed.
They always cut the living ones out first.

Karl Drinkwater

TIME

To the man with dead eyes and a target to meet
I'm just a number
a unit of production
a sentient commodity
now out of time

Pieces of me shrink wrapped and anonymous
the label assuring you
that I lived a happy life
grass fed and free ranged
for a fraction of time

So you eat my corpse, believing the greenwash
that your ethics allowed me
a token of natural life
before being slaughtered
long before time

You love your dog and want to save the whale
While my flesh marinates
And your husband salivates
At how I'll melt in his mouth
Come dinner time.

Perhaps someday you'll make the connection
that a pig is a dog
is a whale is a life
that we all want to live
Maybe, in time.

Nicola McLean

IF ONLY…

If only you could see me
I'm a sister, just like you
I'm a daughter and good friend
And I would be a great Mum too

If only you would let me
Keep my baby by my side
Instead he's killed at five days old
It's called infanticide!

If only you wouldn't steal the milk
I produce for my little boy
I wouldn't be a prisoner
And my baby would be my joy

If only everyone could see
The atrocities that are wrought
Each and every day here
Before your milk is bought

If only you would put compassion
Before putting MY milk in your tea
It is NOT about your likes and wants
It's about my babies' deaths and ME

If only we were free to live
Our lives as we were meant
But humans force us all to 'live'
A life of hell and vile torment!

Susan Buckland

PERCY

Percy pig is sad today,
Because his friend was taken away,
Bundled in a truck with no goodbye,
Percy has to wonder why.
Is he going with the others to a new abode?
A pig sty mansion down the road,
Will he have fresh mud and lots of hay?
Will he be happy and play all day.
But then Percy sniffs and starts to cry,
Because deep down he knows the reason why,
There'll be no fresh mud; there will be no more hay,
For tomorrow it is slaughter day.
His friend is on his way to die,
To be made into sausage, bacon and pork pie,
All because man's greed knows no end,
Percy must grieve the death of his friend.
But his grief won't last long, just the rest of his life;
Because soon, it will be his turn to meet the knife.

Nicola Alexandra Evans

COVENTRY

I stand for hours in the cold.
Cold? No colder than you, with the ice wind coming in through the slats of the lorry.
I try to get nearer to the fire, among the crowd.
But crowded and jammed among other calves, you would rather have space.
I smell the smoke - everything smells of smoke.
You smell fear all around you, ready to become panic again at the next stop.

Then
your truck is sighted.

Everything here becomes chaos, the painful feeling in my chest grows. Everyone near you panics, but there is no room to run, your chests crushed together.

Then
your truck passes.

I don't notice that I'm crying.
Because I heard all of you crying.
It'll haunt me forever.

Karl Drinkwater

PLEASE SIR

Please sir, where's my baby?
My milk is meant for him
No such thing as happy cows
The reality is grim

Please sir, I've had so many calves
All taken away from me
I'm sore, I'm sick and tired
Hooked up to machinery

Please sir, acknowledge my life
my desire to just be
I'm more than the sum of my parts
Not just a commodity.

Please sir, I'm just a new-born
Not a waste product as you say
I'm scared and weak and tiny
A life lived for just one day

Please sir, look me in the eye
meet my gaze and see,
Just once before you end my life,
The soul that lives in me.

Please sir, please, bear witness
As I tremble now in fear
My young life for a carton of milk
The disconnect is clear.

Nicola McLean

THE BEAST

Asleep, I dream of days gone by
 - of grass, and trees, and open sky,
 of company I chose to keep,
 while playing at my mother's feet…

But like the calm before the storm,
 the dream takes on a different form.
 Enter the "Beasts", with sticks of thunder,
 I cannot help but stop and wonder.

Mother, she stands up, and cries,
 and looks the Beasties in their eyes.
 Young and brave and fears no one,
 but never having seen a gun.

The beasts take aim, and open fire,
 one more shot, a little higher…

…Mother she is silent now.
 One beast lets out a whooping "wow!"

…

In my den of concrete and steel,
 My senses tell me this is for real.
 The beasts they came that one sad day,
 and took my other life away.

I look around my prison cell,
the beasts approach, I sense their smell.
Outside my cage they stand and stare,
I try to act like they're not there.
Nowhere to run, nowhere to hide,
the constant staring hurts my pride.
I pace in fury, utter rage.
no escape from this damned cage!

...

... Enters the beast who comes each day,
to clean my mess and scraps away.
It gives me food, and sweeps my cell,
and likes to think it treats me well.

All these years of humiliation and pain,
when will freedom come again?
But what's this? The door's ajar!
Thoughts of dreams and worlds afar.

I seize my chance and make a dash,
only to be stopped by the beasts whiplash.
Turning I snarl and bite its arm.
It turns and shouts of bodily harm.

People watch in wide-eyed awe,
 as the keeper hits the floor.
 "Get some help, it's just too bad!
 The Beast she's gone a raving mad!"

Men arrive with no delay,
 and shoot and shoot and shoot away.
 "Beast, oh Beast, oh Beast!!" They cry,
 as slowly, the lioness, does die.

Mango Wodzak

EMPATHY ENZYME

Taking out a pound of flesh,
Cooked and scarred, they say it's fresh.
Knives eager cutting and ripping.
Sauces on the side for dipping.

Dracula's brown chunk, can't walk,
It's marked for mocking, impaled on a fork.
Lifted to the mouth empowered,
The journey leaving angels deflowered.

Chewed into nothing, gulped down.
Going forth to tour a terrifying town.
Going down the message is said,
The flesh of another finds a bed.

Strangely the stranger, imparting dreams.
Suddenly aloud the eater screams.
Fresh experiences absorbed inside,
The enzymes of nutrition hide.

The man is soaking up the life,
But only the one of mind – its strife.
The flesh has no nutrition to add,
Or a dominant ego to pad.

The experiences now are part of the eater,
A crappy life lived in less than a metre.
All like the memories had happened to him,
Even conscious, they removed his limb.

The beatings, the scars, the aches from no room,
The human choosing what goes in and out the womb.
No communication, family or friends,
Force fed so heavy, the body bends.

The exhaustion and thirst, cramped in a truck,
Buried alive in all our own muck.
So many miles, we were there,
Our enhanced noses smell hell in the air.

Whipped and yelled into a writhing pen.
The screams and cries are not from men.
Wanting retreat, but there's no space,
Anticipation of terror fills this place.

Like my peers before, I'm jabbed ahead,
Here I see how many are dead,
The cry of the dying call out,
But people continue merciless and stout.

The floor is slippery and dark red,
I see a man's eyes, pronouncing me dead.
An object crashed through my throat,
Splurging blood like a flooded boat.

The agonising murder here
The eater feels all, but is alive and dear.
He just experienced through his eye,
The horrific moment he did die.

Chemical memory like a leech,
Wonders why the stomach had to teach.
But now there is a shared past,
With who he had for dinner last.

The reminders, memories, continue on.
The eater stopped just knowing one.
The life of one he's now combined.
Their experiences intertwined.

Each night nightmares came,
"I'll never eat something dead again."

Robbie Nuwanda

WHAT BECAME OF YOU MY BELOVED?

On an early winter's morning
I was out walking with my friend
The mists rose up from the paddocks
Illuminated by the soft glow
Of the first rays of sun.

In the distance I could hear
The barking of dogs
The sound of a gun.

Suddenly, out across the field
I spied a panicked faun.
She ran frantically back and forth
Not sure which way to run.

I stopped in my tracks in anguish
My heart was captured with great grief.
"Over here!" I called to her
"To the forest, you'll be safe!"

I don't think that she heard me
As the hounds were drawing in.
Their rapid footsteps drummed a warning
Their approach came from both sides.

Her hasty breaths were visible in the frosty air
She had to make a choice
As the hounds came bounding into view
She darted through the fence.

What became of you my beloved?
Did fortune smile upon you that day?
Or did they shoot you dead
Cut off your head
And mount it on a wall?
Did they slice your glorious body into pieces?
So that all that was left of you was a morsel of meat
Chewed up, swallowed and forgotten?

No, I can't forget you
Nor the fear for you that shook my heart
And I cannot help but call the hunters what they are –
The terrorists of the countryside.

Emma Letessier

Catch of the day
Glass octopus lies broken
sea angels fleshy wings arrested
Miles long nets drag incidental catch
indiscriminate murder

Catch of the day
gasping mouths breathing noxious air
rapidly vacant eyes reflecting an alien
planet of cloud and sky
lobsters boiled alive claws clacking helplessly
shrimp still moving frozen to death or beheaded

sea food

surf
    and
        turf

           shrimp salad

the myth of sustainable agriculture
                q
                u
                a

This is how we rape a planet

CATCH OF THE DAY

Nancy Correa

DEVIL'S SHORES

There's a gathering storm over Paradise
An evil banished from Hell, left to its own device
When the meaning of ethics is torn apart by semantics
We're left to fight a cancer in the Atlantic

We let our toes hang off the edge of the Earth
An island where blood is spilled to prove a man's worth
Armed to the teeth with the passion, to keep suffering in fashion
An ultimatum sent to the front door of compassion

The sea sings her song to an audience on the shore
A plea for peace like it once was before
Where we heard a cry for help, too loud to ignore
They heard an invitation for a declaration of war

We're waiting in silence for the screams to begin
The two-legged devils, the shame of all our kin
A cultural carnage, a tradition of slaughter
We'll never forgive them for spilling blood in the water

Lenny Marignier

THRESHER
Squalus vulpinus

Let us craft carpets from marine debris.
Let us slough off
our Styrofoam greed for bowls of fin soup,
using gritty insistence instead
of microbeads. Let us fix a filter
to our washing machines
to prevent our nano-fibres reaching
the sea and begetting synthetic herring
and anchovies. Let us unlay
the cables that derange
your electro-receptors.
Let us fill gillnets
with nothing but the will to steeply increase
your numbers. Let us weep
no more mermaids' tears. Let us
leap clear of our pelagic fear
that it's too late to change.
Let us mount a campaign to un-purse
the seine. Let us generate and
maintain a higher internal purpose
than that of our surrounds. Let
us herd our diurnal urge for PVC
into a shoal and stun it
with one thrash of our faith
in your recovery. Let us prey
only on apathy.

Susan Richardson

FETCH
Squalus acanthius

If we train her to *Wait!*, might she fail
to migrate and evade
all slavering trawlers?

Can we teach her to retrieve the past,
which used to   bounce   when we threw it,
before the deepest
                    plunge
in her numbers?

Will she learn to bury our bony blunders
in the mud of the sea floor
and will her back's toxic spines,
like hackles, rise,
when anyone tries to exhume them?

If we refuse to use *Rock Salmon* –
the alias we gave her for edible appeal –
will she feel more inclined to come to our side
when called?

If we decline to believe we could improve her breed -
(whiter spots, smoother skin, primped fins,
limpid eyes), will she never be demeaned
by the prize of Best In Show?

Might she fertilise our hearts when she dies?
Not hauled on a longline.
Just, finally, old.

Susan Richardson

SPRINGTIME

As in a perfect fairy tale
That brings such sweet delight
'Neath blossom boughs and blackbirds
Springtime curls up tight
Waiting to uncoil
In the freshly furrowed earth
And wriggle through the raindrops
Into sunlight and rebirth

But there's something disconnected
Within these perfect hills
As snow-white lambs leap about
All waiting to be killed
And sleepy sheep ruminate
Whilst tourist ramblers laugh
And take out flask and camera
For a pretty photograph
Meanwhile behind a sprawling hedge
Out of sight and mind
A dairy herd stands in filth
Well away from prying eyes
And the ramblers ramble on
Through this picture-perfect scenery
With oxtail soup and paté
(A little stain upon the greenery)
Enjoying nature's bounty
But unwilling (or unable)
To stop and think – connect the dots

And see the farming fable
For what it is – a factory line
Of food that no-one needs
Fed by propaganda
And Governmental greed
But rambling on in ignorance
It hardly seems surprising
That the walkers feel some part
Of the earth in splendour rising
> *No need to see the cattle*
> *With swollen, bloody udders*
> *The sheep hung up in chains*
> *Throat open, like the others*
> *In lines and lines of skin and meat*
> *That make up picnic lunches*
> *For ramblers in the fields*
> *Picking daffodils in bunches*

I see this world is beautiful
I see we are connected
But this divisive ugliness
Leaves us *all* dissected into
Those that understand and care
And those who ramble unaware
And those who simply choose to eat
With nothing on their minds but *meat…*

But *surely*

It's no irrationality
 no current, fleeting fashion
To expose the vile banality
 with altruistic passion
And a healthy practicality
 balanced with compassion
To render this barbarity
 A pointless bloody ration
And consign it to the rubbish bin
With all of history's shame
With knife and noose and manacle
And all unnatural pain

And only *then* will springtime be
Enjoyed with sweet delight
It may not be a fairy tale
But at least it will be RIGHT.

Philip McCulloch-Downs

MY FRIEND, MY GIRL, MY GLENDA

Rescued on a summer's day,
The farmer said: "She's spent"
In truth, no longer profitable
Was what that farmer meant.

Your world completely changed that day,
And hey, my world changed too.
Many lessons we learnt together
As our special friendship grew.

Foraging and frolicking,
I adored your sense of fun.
I'd love to sit and watch you ruffling your feathers
Dust-bathing in the sun.

Your frailty was always proof,
Of your past life on the line.
I guess I knew this day would come
But I hoped we'd have more time.

Your bond with your sisters,
So special to see.
An unforgettable friendship
Missed by them and missed by me.

Take your wings and fly, my girl,
And leave me well assured,
That I will always be a voice
Against all that you endured.

You're so much more than an egg.
My friend, my girl, my Glenda.

Honey Morris

the first time she felt the fresh air was too much for her ravaged lungs
and she almost stopped breathing
but she continued inhaling the sweet air redolent with the promise of
verdant spaces and crawling life
she was so frail that what little feathers she did have fell out
making lazy twirls in the dust motes
she slept and breathed and breathed and slept
her thin bones could not hold what little she weighed
the calcium expended for laying eggs stolen day after day
rendered her body with osteoporosis

one day the promise of grass, dirt and sun were too enticing
she finally stood - walking with wobbly, petite steps
a thin dancer lost in her equilibrium
dancing past the memory of stacked cages, ammonia laden air and
dead comrades she moved ahead
parting the dust motes
letting the sun shine on her for the first time

SARAH UNDEFEATED

Nancy Correa

GOAT POWER

Some see me
and think what a cutie
and assume that being cute
is my only duty

some see me and think
of fresh milk & cheeses
or in the nativity
near the tiny baby Jesus

but really us goats
we are so much more
we are dwarf and la mancha
and some of us Boer

I know I may look
like a delicate flower,
but do not underestimate
my immense caprine power

Kat von Cupcake

I USED TO BE A ZOMBIE

I was a zombie, I confess,
I munched all bodies, more or less
I loved those steak and kidney pies,
and as for gravy smothered thighs…
especially with a side of fries!
I'd likely even've eaten their eyes,
if properly glazed and caramelised..

baconed burgers, sausaged dogs, I'd eat the bloodied lot,
hams and spams and baby lambs, I'd eat them cold or hot.

For brekkie lunch and dinner tea,
any corpse at all for me,
I loved all animals equally!
Excepting perhaps the swan and cat,
and dogs too come to think of it…
I was a civil chap of course,
and never dreamt to eat a horse.

yes, I was a zombie one time too,
I ate cadavers just like you!
I ate their backs, I ate their wings,
mostly cooked or fried with other things.
I even ate the offspring, at barely two months young,
and without that plate of devilled eggs, my mornings came unstrung.

But then I woke to what I was,
it made me stop and think because…
well frankly, it just dawned on me,
that sheep and pigs are she and he,
and he and she… It dawned on me.
Not pounds of flesh, nor thats and its,
but inside someone else there sits,
who sees the world, and has their thoughts,
dreams their dreams and worries their warts,
lives their lives, and wants their peace,
not to end up fried in grease.

I recognise the being see,
his individuality,
I looked into a piglet's eyes,
and suddenly I felt chastised,
for the bacon I had eaten, only some short time ago,
it set my thoughts a-thinking, and my heart it set aglow…

from that very moment forth, I ceased my zombie habits
I pushed aside the meateries and breakfasting on rabbits.

I used to be a zombie, I'm glad I am no more,
for the animals which go unseen, I simply can't ignore.

Now all I eat is vegetables,
and fruits and nuts and grains,
but not the little animals.. I recognise their brains.

Mango Wodzak

I DON'T CARE

Why do you care?
He said to me
I'm not being rude, but why?
It's not your responsibility
Whether animals live or die

The planet and population
Will get by on its own, with luck
Leave the worry to someone else
Let them give a fuck

The meat and dairy industry?
Christ! Who gives a toss?
That's what cows are there for
It's MAN who is the boss

I looked at him with interest
His empty human eyes
His ego unassailable
His logic worldly-wise

So - Why do you care?
He said with a grin
When there's nothing that you can do?
Well
I said
I feel I should
So I am not like you

I try to harm no creature
I try because you won't
I care because I can
I said
I care because you don't

So - go back to your burgers
Your babies and your beer
You'll make no earthly difference
However long you're here

But I am bigger than you
He said
And I am everywhere

I looked in his vacuous heart and replied
I know
But
I don't care.

Philip McCulloch-Downs

THE HUNTER

"I am a predator"
He boasted with some pride
As his canine servant
Cowered by his side

"I have a special duty
To keep the populations low
Of pigs, of deer and things that fly
I deal a savage blow

"The farmers are so grateful
They endorse my killing as good sense
It stops the pests from eating their crops
And gives the system balance"

I smiled at his monologue
And really tried my best
To hold my tongue
But there was no way I could let the issue rest

"A predator you call yourself?
I think you are confused
Let's examine this
And then we'll see, this choice of word's misused!

"A true predator has several things
All of which you lack
The only things which you possess
Are guns upon a rack

"Say, pass me your gun, my friend
Let's make the battle fair
Who would win between you and a wild boar?
I think the answer's clear!

"I look at you and fail to see
In any shape or form
Sharp teeth, nor claws, nor talons, sir
For a predator these are the norm

"Another thing before I'm done
Let's talk about agility
If you had to run down your prey in the forest
You severely lack ability

"And despite your dearth of predatory skills
The animals have nowhere left to hide
You have an unfair advantage
With dogs upon your side

"You see it's your troop of rowdy hounds
That really do the work
While you stand around, with gun and wait
You really are a jerk!

"On days long past
These lands were roamed
By wolf, by lynx, by bear
But farmers with their herded lots
Cried, "Get them out of here!"

"It's these animals I think you'll find
Which are the predators true
If it weren't for their expulsion
There'd be no job for you!

"Us humans are a stupid lot
Glorifying mindless killing without need
Animal exploitation isn't necessary
It's a hideous system based on greed

"For many years they told us lies
All of which we believed
If you think we need meat, eggs and dairy
I'm afraid you're still deceived

"So tell me again, my good fellow
What a ferocious predator you are
But based on these conclusions
I'm calling you a liar!"

Emma Letessier

THE DOG IS RUNNING MADLY ROUND THE OFFICE

Rebel dog defying civil servants,
How cool you are, a canine insurgent.
Disrupt the paper pushing and filing,
Endless statistics, ceiling-high piling.
Boxer by name, cauliflower their ears,
And leave the bureaucrats quaking in fear.

Karl Drinkwater

IF ANIMALS SPOKE ENGLISH

if animals spoke English what would they have to say?
"Thank you for the care you give,
and thanks for all the hay"?
"Thank you all for granting this,
Oh so precious gift of life,
it really is so trouble-free,
and void of stress and strife"?
"Thank you for the home you give,
 for keeping wolves at bay,
we just love all you do for us"
Is that just what they'd say?

Would they hold a fête, to celebrate,
free lodging, food and board,
Sing our praises, bow to us,
and offer us reward?

Now let us not all kid ourselves,
with sugarcoated lies,
when really we are breeding them,
to fatten up their thighs...
and rumps and breasts and wings and things,
they cannot live without,
I think it's pretty clear to me,
that this is what they'd shout:

"Those branding irons and docking shears,
these staples to our ears,
They cause us untold suffering, our eyes they bring to tears.
Castration pliers! Now listen squires,
that's not behaving nicely,
I'd like for you to understand, I'll tell it you precisely.

"Surely it is plain to see, subjection to such agony,
leads only to antagony.

"Those pastures green, were rarely seen,
all fairytales and fibs,
and while you gently fool yourself,
your eyes are on our ribs.

"You rape our females on a rack,
and steal our babes asunder,
the cause of so much misery, now is it any wonder,
how unimpressed we are with you,
with all the pain you've put us through,
we'd like to bid you all adieu.

"If the shoe were on the other foot
Now how's it best I this should put?
You'd be up in arms with fury, crying with despair,
screaming bloody murder, and pulling out your hair.

"There is no thanks for us to give,
of that you can be sure,
our lives are full of misery from the hardship we endure.

"Our request to you is simple, and we beg you to comply,
to see us as your brethren, as you look us in the eye,
and cease your wretched habits of the dairy, eggs and flesh,
and think about your food from a mind that is afresh."

Mango Wodzak

NO JOYRIDES

hey jack!
get off my back
what makes you think
I want to feel your butt crack?

how would you feel
if folks jumped on you?
and rode you around
instead of walking on the ground?

do you think it's okay that
into my sides your heels jab?
if you want transportation
go call a cab

science has proven,
the pain that it brings
so quit with the riding
of other living things

Kat von Cupcake

A VEGAN FROM SLOUGH

A vegan called Jessie from Slough

tried hard to avoid any row

but folk gave her grief,

said, *"Don't you miss beef?"*

She said, *"Not as much as the cow."*

Dominic Berry

THE VEGAN TROLL

I call myself 'The Vegan Troll'
I like to make a fuss
By commenting on people's Facebook posts
"Mmmm, hummus!"

You could post a photo of your new born babe
Or a gripe about your day
It matters not to me what you choose to share
I'll comment anyway

I use every opportunity to remind them all
That animals have feelings too
And say things like: "How do you know someone's an omni?
"Don't worry they'll tell you!"

And although my trolling infuriates
And carries little wit
Really, I can't help myself
I guess seitan made me do it!

Emma Letessier

SILLY ME

Would you let us put
Your baby in a box and
Lie it on a blanket
With its cage door locked?
What if we gave it bedding
Some water and a light
And changed its dirty nappy
Almost every single night?
Would you let us give it pills
And keep it warm and dry?
And feed it 'til it's fat
And ignore it when it cries?
Would you care if we kept it
For all its little life?
Until we take it out
And put it to the knife?

Oh,
Thank *God* for little babies
All small and fat and cheap...

But, of course, it's not *your* baby

Silly me -
It's just meat

Philip McCulloch-Downs

PEACHES

There was a young lady called Peaches,
who simply loved animals to pieces.
She ate pigs and sheep,
and for cows she would weep,
when baked in a sauce of rich greases.

Mango Wodzak

MARY HAD A LITTLE LAMB

Mary had a little Lamb,
she also had tomatoes,
she covered them in greasy sauce,
and fried them with potatoes.

Mango Wodzak

NUTTY

I'm a vegan. I'm nuts, people say.
I'm a brazil, all big and creamy.
I'm a cashew with this fabulous curve in the middle.

My enemies say, 'She's peanut butter.
She goes with anything.'

Well, I am a bit of a (*waggles bosom*) chest-nut.
I'm also Nut, the Egyptian goddess of the sky.
Just a little short of worshippers.

When in love, I pine, right to my kernel.
Now don't take the pistachio.
Nothing can crush me though –
like an almond, when stomped on
I just become delicious marzipan.
I would be willing to live between
Christmas cake and icing.

The weakest go to the walnut
and no pecan.
I know, I'm completely conkers.
But as fragrant as a coconut
and as hard to get to the core of;
as nibbly as chocolate peanuts
that you just want more of.

I'm a vegan. I'm a nut.
And no, life doesn't get samier.
Which is a really rubbish rhyme for the best nut of all –
Macadamia!

Cathy Bryant

COMFORT FOOD

my wife makes celestial
French toast. thick slices,
fried with frothy banana batter
(not stolen hen's eggs)

on the side, juicy cuts
of tempeh bacon. smoky flax meat
soaks up sticky drippy syrup
(precious porcine back fat remains
with its intended owner)

two cups of coffee in two favorite mugs
mine, black. hers, sweetened
with pure white coconut cream
(no forced udder output here)

breakfast with her
is a prayer, a ritual
for eating

the way Nature intended:
from her body
(not theirs)

Linda Monahan

THE MYTH OF PROTEIN

It is a biochemical compound
whose name Berzelius found.
Von Voit claimed, *"Flesh makes flesh."*
Sanger sequenced insulin,
Purutz prized haemoglobin
and the Swedish were impressed.

More studies on its benefits
directed mutagenesis
as Weissman had foreseen.
To give their claims such credence
does not distract from this grievance:
"Where do vegans get protein?

What exactly can you eat?
Can't be healthy, with no meat."
Such Shakespearian introspection.
Between the facts to delve,
lament, *"B12 or not B12,*
Surely that *must be the question?"*

It's simple eating sensible.
The soy bean lacks cholesterol,
is easily fortified
and cooked can taste exceptional
(tongue-tinglingly sensual)
and, yes, it will provide

protein! (as will peanut butter,
black beans, flax seeds, pecans, almonds,
lentils and cashews)
And yet, here is *my* beef;
hearing debate on my *belief*,
people questioning what I *choose*.

I don't *choose* for pigs to feel.
Don't just *believe* their pain is real.
It's fact. Not myth. Not needed.
Can we, in evolution,
swap our myths for resolution,
see this cruelty superseded?

The facts of protein's chemistry,
documents throughout history,
are laid out plain and clear
but still, I hopefully wait
for that honest, heartfelt date
when protein's myths will finally
disappear.

Dominic Berry

VEGAN IS THE FOOD OF LOVE

We've all seen the gourmets
eating salmon mornays,
judging and quibbling with a fine insouciance;
their food bred in pain and dirt always,
and served in healthless sauces for a posh-bred response.
No, I'm a vegan. My food is full of joy and fun,
chestnut bourguignon tingling the tongue,
red pepper hummus in a fresh-baked bun
served with sprouts either Brussels or mung.
Chocolate mousse with whisky, and yes, tofu.
I won't apologise for what's good for you.
Asparagus spears, tips glistening with dressing,
fragrant pomegranates, our senses caressing,
- chicken burgers are seriously unprepossessing;
the fatty squeezings of the bovine mammary gland
– distressing and depressing.
Bring me a cake, and a mango, and a kiss.
From the cruelty and lies, we'll find solace.

Cathy Bryant

INGREDIENTS

Vanilla hazelnut ice cream,
unsweetened cocoa powder,
coconut whipped cream, almond milk,
My gut growls *even* louder.
Chilled brewed coffee, dump it in,
whip up this frosted confection.
Pour it in a frigid glass,
Vegan milkshake perfection.

Charles Waters

THE VEGAN MACHO NACHO SECRET

Let me tell you a little secret about how to make a nacho

We make them big like a man so better call 'em macho

It starts with 1 pack vegan mexi-style ground meat crumbles

On the stove in a pan…

What, did I hear your stomach grumble?

One average sized onion, now all sliced

With fire roasted tomatoes in a can all diced

Add a can of corn 'cause you know it will be sweet

Now two tablespoons of garlic will knock you off your feet

Cook it up and set aside, now we're moving on

The next ingredients are all new and need to get along

In a baking dish, thirteen by nine sprayed with cooking oil

Once you get a taste of this masterpiece you know you will be loyal

Break out some white corn chips and layer them nice and even

Then pull out the can opener 'cause now it's time to begin

Open up a can of refried pintos, then wipe your hands on your jeans

Add some veggie chili, some kidneys and then some black beans

Now for some fun layer vegan shredded pepper jack

Then because you can, some vegan cheddar! Whaddya think 'bout dat?

Next, repeat everything I just said to make it a double layer

Then slap it in the oven for 20 @ 350 then say a little prayer

That these Macho Nachos might fill the bodies and minds of all God's children

And that the prophecy be fulfilled that they will come because you build them

Once you smell them pull them out then jump up and down and give a shout

Declare to the world that the Nachos are complete

And tell all the people that it's finally time to eat.

But not before we add all the final toppers

That make this gift from God a true show stopper

Green onion chopped is the perfect garnish

Then add some salsa hot enough to remove some varnish

To cool the tongue and keep our taste buds lubed

Some veggie sour cream and an avocado cubed

Now that it's finished and with joy your guests are weeping

Commit this poem to memory it's a secret well worth keeping

Marc McGowan

FRUIT NOT FLESH

Why chickens, sheep and pigs,
when there's kiwifruit and figs?
Why turkeys, cows and fish,
when there's oranges delish?

I cannot get the thought you see,
to fathom this mentality,
of killing half grown animals,
and gorging on the internals,
while such a lot of other things,
nature us so freely brings.

We need not chew on someone's leg,
nor fry up someone else's egg,
nor deal someone a bloody hack,
to thinly slice and dice their back.

No, we've got fruit to eat you see,
offered freely by the tree,
no one needs to lose their life,
by brutal steely butcher knife.

There's apples, pears and rambutans,
and chempadeks and durians,
or delightfully purple cherries,
n' other fruit confectioneries...

We don't need all those cages,
it's been like this for ages,
those booths and stalls and branding,
and callous heavy handling!

Now it's time for something new,
so push aside cadaver stew,
for since the time we left our wombs,
we've used our bodies much like tombs
a habit which has surely caused,
atrocities we've barely paused,
to reflect upon and see the truth
that slaughtering someone in their youth,
to feast upon their flesh's... uncouth!

Fruit you see, it's meant to be,
the food for me, and she and he.. and thee!

Mango Wodzak

A GAY VEGAN LIMERICK

A vegan called Dom from round here
said, *"Please, can you not call me 'queer'?
I just love chickpeas
and tahini, so, please,
I'm a hummus-sexual, my dear."*

Dominic Berry

EARTH ANGELS

Earth angels dancing to the catatonic rhythm of denial
They speak of love and light and of compassion
Over the corpses of animals tortured and confined
On their plates
As they tell you that they are here to serve a higher purpose
You can't help but wonder what higher purpose they are serving as their guts are full of suffering and violence created and manufactured especially for them
And yet they look at you and speak to you with eyes of innocence, certain that their kindness is over-flowing into every spiritual realm of truth that could possibly exist
You can't help but wonder if most everyone around you is crazy or there are just some forms of life that you will never understand

Atara Schimmel

The moon's silvery gaze awakens something within me
and I turn just in time to see her lidless gaze seeming
to wink as clouds obscure her
I reveal my body to her as I hear one of
her creatures howl into the argent night
In the place where penumbra becomes light I see the wolf
she howls for those trapped
she howls for those beaten
she howls for her dead family
she howls for those poisoned
poisoned as the earth is poisoned
the wolf stops to inhale the heady night
has she caught the scent of my herbivore breath?
I sit vulnerable hairless prey
she comes closer
I look into those fathomless luminescent eyes
I extend my hand

Nancy Correa

WOLFEN ME

AWAKE Part I

Tiny fingers curled tight shut
A body that's cold and pale
You hope to see him let out a yawn
and run like others his age.
"How can this be?" you say with pain
It's easy to forget -
while life can leave a body forever
the innocence always stays.
"Nature is kinder than the will of Man",
you say as he leaves the sand.
While men hold on to guns and laws,
the waves took him by hand.
When home was but a forgotten dream
and hope turned to despair,
the waves knew no race, no colour, no creed,
took him where he'd be safe.
"No more", you say.
"Just let them live"
You hope love will prevail
You beg, you plead, implore with tears
No difference does it make.

You raise your voice, protest and fight
Your shouts begin to weak
Out of deep slumber a shallow voice
disgruntled, slowly speaks,
"I do as I please. My choice to claim.
My choice to hurt. My choice to kill.
Now shhh, go back to sleep!"

A tribute to Aylan Kurdi

Gunjan Bhatia

AWAKE Part II

She follows her pack with playful glee
Her playground, the big, wide sea.
She spins and leaps, and laughs out loud
What joy to swim with family!
But soon, the open path they chose,
begins to close right in.
They circle on in search of escape
while spears and knives pierce in.
The air is filled with cries of pain
Their panic turns to dread
One by one, lives start to fall
The blue begins to red.
She fights and sees her loved ones pass
and then is dragged away
Her laughter controlled by commands and tricks
Her new home - a manmade cell
She weeps her life away while Man,
applauds and pats himself
"Nature is kinder than the will of Man",
but there is no nature there.
"No more", you say.
"Just let them live"

You hope love will prevail
You beg, you plead, implore with tears
No difference does it make.
You raise your voice, protest and fight
Your shouts begin to weak
Out of deep slumber a shallow voice
disgruntled, slowly speaks,
"I do as I please. My choice to claim.
My choice to hurt. My choice to kill.
Now shhh, go back to sleep!"

In honor of the dolphins being captured and killed in Taiji, Japan and all beings in captivity. Special tribute to 'Angel', the stolen albino dolphin from the 2014 Taiji hunt.

Gunjan Bhatia

AWAKE Part III

She knows him well, the hand that feeds
She thinks he loves her back
She waits for him, come rain, come shine
He is all she's ever had.
He took her calf, he takes her milk
Maybe it was her fault
Maybe next time it will be better,
and she can raise her own.
He speaks kind words, though not to her
She hears a truck outside
He drags her out and forces her in,
but then, does not look back.
She smells the fear from miles away
The truck comes to a halt.
She wants to know he'll be outside
to make this journey stop.
She waits in line...afraid to breathe
The air is thick with death
She hears the clatter of heavy machines
Her hooves begin to skid.
"Nature is kinder than the will of man"
She finally does submit

Sometimes the only way to freedom
Is to let life slowly drip.
"No more", you say.
"Just let them live"
You hope love will prevail
You beg, you plead, implore with tears
No difference does it make.
You raise your voice, protest and fight
Your shouts begin to weak
Out of deep slumber a shallow voice
disgruntled, slowly speaks,
"I do as I please. My choice to claim.
My choice to hurt. My choice to kill.
Now shhh, go back to sleep!"

For the countless beings whose lives and deaths we control every day.

Gunjan Bhatia

FOR WHITE VEGANS WHO CLAIM THE FLESH OF OTHERS

it is not an ornament for display / for appraisal / for praise / but my body
is a treasure chest / a small room containing the greatest versions
of myself / and well that's it / and well shit / there is literally
no space left to stow your drivel

and do not mistake my body for your own / it is not your science
project / do not monitor its fuel and activity / my body has no desire
to move like your body does / to look like your body does / or act
or sound like your body does / have you seen my body? have you
seen what it can do? without you? have you seen how it can move?
in ways impossible for your body? how it unwinds for itself? floats
for itself? rejoices and promises for itself? and not for you?

and my body's space is immeasurable / its ratios are a cosmic perfection
there are galaxies on my thighs and a nova on my tongue / you cannot
contain me / you should know this by now:

Do not hurt my body.

Do not bend it over itself and crumple it.

Do not rip down its gates and creep inside.

Do not shove your knuckles in.

Do not sink your teeth in.

Do not batter it; pummel it, spit upon it.

Do not remove its clothing and whip it.

Do not tie it to your bumper and drag it.

Do not chuckle at it. Do not smother it.

Do not glare or wag your finger or tisk-tisk it.

Do not string it up in a tree or clothe it with the robe of birds.

Do not burn it. Do not chokehold it. Do not aim and shoot (and shoot and shoot and shoot) at my body.

My body is papered
in ancient velvet so surely
it is royal enough to matter.

Sea Sharp

KINDLY

There are cases where a fact cannot come at all
and a leaf falls
down in front of me
and I steal this leaf
because I need it
and don't want to think
about the future.
Just this leaf.
By looking at it.
Looking at it
regularly, then maybe
under a microscope.
Hours pass in this fashion.
When you got your first microscope
do you remember
how it came with four or five blank slides
packed in Styrofoam
and because you couldn't resist
you picked your freshest scab
or ran the slide across your finger
so you could see
inside your own blood? Love
is an emergency.
And every decimal of dew is.
And every time that we are careless.

———

Love is an emergency
that slips like a deer
from the wound of Christ
to land on the water
without bitterness
in a glister of accident
and won't think twice
about climbing that tiny staircase again
in ice
to board a plane
again to fly
back into the kiss
of the same disaster

no recompense
no flotation device

the kind of suicide mission
where you're not even free
after you've died

like how

when you hang yourself
in prison
they cuff you
before they cut you
down.

———

Attaching a bird wing
to a fishing line and pole
and dragging it along the ground
trains hounds to trace game.
The name of the game
is kill what you love.
The name of the game
is kill what you hate.
The wings are bait
to teach the dogs to love their fate
which is to find what someone great
shot out
of the sky forever
and point: and it's my heart
that is the convict.
I have to get the convict
what he wants.

———

Someone dressed as Santa
shoots everyone
at the Christmas party,
beginning with the child
who answers the door.
Santa shoots everyone
then self.

In Spain, swordfish in the sea
do the seguidilla
and some make youthful mistakes
and some guffaw
and some are forced into slavery
and some are bedsore.

Some have beauty that is obscene.

We work in shifts
to be equivalent.

He was happy one minute.

12 a.m. to 12:01:
everyone turns to everyone
in their sequined dress
in a snow of silver dots
and kisses everyone's champagne
moustache.

Someone's false eyelash
floating in everyone's glass
can only be distinguished
as unwishable and untrue
by the tiny bead of glue
that had been holding it in place.

You reach for my face.

A leaf falls down.

It is a featherless bone;
it is the sound of steel on stone;
it is the siren in the dial tone
rinsing out your brain before bed.
The leaf is green but it is red
in the microscope.
When all words contained all others, I said, I hope.

Ashley Capps

NATURE

That man eats meat, is part of nature,
no one should deny,
a bear eats fish and cats eat mice,
Need one to ask why?

That man seeks shelter, from the sun,
and from the wind that blows,
no one really looks confused,
that's just the way things goes.

He clears a glade, amidst the trees,
and cultivates the land.
He has to eat if he'll survive,
everyone can understand.

He builds a house, upon a hill,
which soon becomes a town,
we're a social lot we human race,
and no one gives a frown.

Mankind, we use our little minds,
which nature us did grant,
and with it we design and scheme,
a nuclear power plant.

It is through nature, that we learn,
and build and probe you see,
how else would it have come about,
this elec-trici-ty?

Sewage? That's a dirty lot,
let's dump it in the sea.
What else are we to do with it?
It's just a tiny fee.

We make mistakes, but who's to blame?
It happens all the time,
Which makes it very difficult,
to judge just what's a crime.

Humans we are but far from perfect,
I think we must agree,
that nature it has brought about,
a natural catastrophe.

The moral of this story is,
"it's nature" is no excuse.
Think about just what you do,
and ask, "Is this abuse?"

Mango Wodzak

WE WILL

We will always be mindful to spread the word
that the vegan ideal crowns all we have heard.
Our respect for animals will guide what we say.
We will express what we know in a gentle way.
We will be examples of the nonviolence we preach,
so that people can witness new heights they can reach.
We will serve justice and summon 'sentient rights'
We will bear witness to all oppressed; and their plights.

We will prepare and share tasty food vegans eat;
rich in vibrant color; both savory and sweet.
With our food and our stamina being so good,
people will see that they haven't understood
how important it is for our diet to evolve,
and the planetary problems we could resolve.
For a plant-powered diet will magically bring
a multitude of benefits to everything.

We will strive to expand our heartfelt compassion
until loving animals is world-wide fashion.
We won't pay for by-products like "blood and bone",
but will make our gardens veganically-grown.
We will read the ingredients before we buy;
Our dollars won't demand an animal to die.
We will protest 'animal use' with each passing year
until every animal can live free of fear.

We won't give up, until that longed-for day arrives
when it's inconceivable to exploit other lives.
There will come a time, when people will wonder how
one could earn their "living" by slaughtering a cow.
We will bring about change; a vegan new age
where the innocent are free from human rage.
Heading for a time when speciesism will cease,
We will live vegan, and produce a world of peace.

M. *"Butterflies" Katz*

I WILL TAKE YOU TO THE SUNSHINE

I will take you to the sunshine.

I will take you to the rivers.

I will take you to the flowers.

I will take you to the streams, the forests, the open spaces.

I will watch you as you love and feed your babies.

I will sit in silence and in awe of you.

I will watch and my heart will be filled with a new faith in humankind and with a new faith in this world.

Will you let me sit beside you?

Will you let me feel the warmth of your presence?

Will you forgive me?

Will you befriend me?

Will you kiss me with your gentle kindness?

I will learn humility.

I will learn compassion.

I will learn how to forgive myself for having hurt you too.

Will you bless me, bless me with you sacred spirit?

Oh, how I yearn to return to you.

Atara Schimmel

On this night when the wind howls its discontent

the silver goddess surveys the carnage before her and weeps

for the two legged

for the four legged

for the cloven hoofed

for the upright ones who decimate their brethren

wolfsbane penny royal petit grain

she casts her argent spell

that chimes the slow death knell

Nancy Correa

WOLF MOON

MY PLEDGE

I pledge that I will work towards a future,
Where cows and sheep aren't seen as bits of meat
Where grain is used instead to feed the hungry,
The starving children begging on the street.
Where sharks and rays aren't threatened with extinction,
and fish can feed forever free from man.
Where kids will learn that tuna live in water
and don't begin their journey in a can.

Our children need to learn that birds have feelings,
including those that Aussies know as chooks.
And humans cause decay and mass extinction
Where rhino aren't just something found in books.
Where milk is something mothers make for babies.
Another species' milk is not for you.
That beef and pork will fill you full of cancer.
The animals' revenge is sad but true.
That eggs are meant to hatch in nests in forests,
and baby boy birds aren't destroyed at birth.
As sure as eggs we slash and burn and murder.
A mindless, bloody blight upon the Earth.
If we're the smartest species on the planet,
Why can't we learn to live without the killing?
Why can't we worship wildlife we encounter?
A wondrous world awaits us if we're willing.

Keith Lupton

HOMECOMING

Walk gently on this Earth
Lest she forget the sound of your breath
behind the force of your wants,
and the web of connection tear so far
that you lose yourself and your place in it.

Walk gently on this Earth
So your spirit may still know
the comforts of home
So your heart may sing
the songs of the birds,
and your hands may remember
how to heal,
not hurt.

Walk gently on this Earth
For you are made of her.
The rivers are your blood,
the trees your bones,
and the animals of this world
your reflection.

Walk gently on this Earth
So you may still have a place to rest,
when you become the wind.

Gunjan Bhatia

HEART OVERHEAD

You can say I never truly lived, but you can't say I never loved.
I've felt it in special, savored moments that were never mine at all.
I told myself to ignore it, and, yes, keep it hidden and gloved.
Yet it was stronger than me, an ocean over a dam, a total landfall.

Ice within melted. Reels of fantasy swirled and collided to a blur.
A sunken, old bed in squalor became a queen's sweet bed of roses.
Only he would never be with me. My roar faded to a weak purr.
What I had of him became less, but I reached for blazing chances.

How It changed every cell and the path blood takes to my heart!
Either it now runs the way to freedom or courage is a bladed curse.
You can't wish yourself into being loved; that's the hardest part.
He was a dahlia or bird of paradise, while I was just a shepherd's purse.

Loving him broke my heart while managing to heal it ever so thoroughly.
My eyes somehow opened along with my heart, spirit, soul, and mind.
That's the nature of true compassion for every living being for an infinity.
I slowly learned to love myself as much as I loved animals of every kind.

I wasn't living up to my ethics when I acted with hatred towards myself,

So, the umbrella of compassion I extend to others no longer excludes me.

I go on loving and am far from being the girl who was close to killing herself.

I have volumes of wisdom still to gain, but in moments I'm now carefree.

I celebrate my imperfect shell that houses an imperfect inner being.

But I carry a concern and love deeper than any doubt or insecurity.

I wear a hard-earned crown of confidence as I savor simply existing.

My eternal love is now requited since it circles right back to me.

Robin Raven

FOR THE FREEDOM AND PEACE OF ALL BEINGS ON EARTH

To the quail and the raven and the white barn owl:
> We give thanks, ask protection, send love.

To the deer and the fox and the great brown bear:
> We give thanks, ask protection, send love.

To the frog and the lizard and the small silent snail:
> We give thanks, ask protection, send love.

To the pine and the poppy and the deep dark earth:
> We give thanks, ask protection, send love.

To the rain and the rivers and the wild open ocean:
> We give thanks, ask protection, send love.

We are kin.
We are kin.
We are sacred,
sacred kin.

Together we walk these mountain sides,
and together we take our rest.
To the mothers and the fathers and the sound-sleeping babes:
> together, let's tend this nest.

This nest of Earth,
this place we all dream,
and learn, and eat, and grow.
Let us build on it carefully,
guard it with love,
teach our hatchlings
all that we know:

>   all we know of least harm,
>   all we know of compassion,
>   all we know of putting our hearts into action.

Coexistence, some say.
Eco-conscious, say others.
But in truth it's no more
than our one sacred nest,
f u l l   o f   l o v e
for our sisters and brothers.

For the freedom and peace of all beings on Earth: Blessed Be.

Linda Monahan

VEGAN PAGAN PRAYER

Lord of the forest and field, Lady of the starlit night,
I acknowledge the truth that for me to live, something must die.
I give thanks for the gift of free will,
And I acknowledge the responsibility that comes with the freedom of choice.
I choose then to abstain from the cycle of unnecessary suffering.
I pledge to be an agent of healing, not a bystander to slaughter.
I say to the animals:
You do not have to suffer and die for me.
I say to the workers:
You do not have to kill for me.
I say to the corporate death machine:
You will no longer profit from my blindness.
I say to the Earth, and to all that is holy,
That though we are taught to feast upon war,
I choose to lay down the sword
And take in peace instead.
I ally myself with Nature, not as her master, but as her child.
I will not claim dominion over that which is wiser than I.
Lord of the forest and field, Lady of the starlit night,
May compassion fulfil and transform me
May I give as You give, may I love as You love
And may my choices bring grace to my life
As You bring grace to the world.
So mote it be.

Dianne Sylvan

POEM CONTRIBUTORS

Alizée Ventderrmidi
Alizée Ventderrmidi is a young Canadian woman from Montreal who cultivates a passion for nature and its contemplation. As a student in literature, she considers herself an explorer. Letting her feelings and perceptions guide her mind, Alizée finds herself in the unknown most of the time. This is her precious way of living. To her, being vegan is to stand for love and harmony.

Anthony Rhead
Anthony Rhead is a passionate vegan. For 18 years he suffered with chronic pain and depression, yet as a consequence of becoming vegan, his life has taken a turn for the better. It inspired him to write poetry and start a small photography business. His perspective has completely altered and he wishes to do whatever he can to share his wonderful experience.

Ashley Capps
Ashley Capps holds an M.F.A. in Poetry from the University of Iowa Writers' Workshop. Her first book of poems is *Mistaking the Sea for Green Fields*. The recipient of a 2011 National Endowment for the Arts Fellowship, she works as a freelance writer and editor for Free from Harm, A Well-Fed World, and other non-profits focused on animal justice and vegan advocacy. She is completing a second collection of poems. Her website is ashley-capps.tumblr.com.

Atara Schimmel
Atara Schimmel is a creative and expressive arts therapist, an artist, a poet and a passionate vegan. Atara dedicates her talents to raising awareness about the prevalence of chronic pain conditions and animal liberation. Atara's award-winning art activism has been featured in newspapers, magazines, blogs and collaborative projects such as The Metrowest Daily News, Disability Issues, the Interstitial Cystitis Network and The Art of Compassion Project. www.ataraschimmel.com

Cathy Bryant
Cathy Bryant has been vegan since 1999, and has previously written for The Vegan magazine. She has won 24 literary awards, and her work has appeared in over 250 publications. Cathy's books are 'Contains Strong Language and Scenes of a Sexual Nature', 'Look at All the Women' and 'How to Win Writing Competitions'. See her listings for skint writers at www.compsandcalls.com. Cathy lives in Cheshire, UK.

Charles Waters
Charles Waters is a children's poet, actor and educator who has performed in schools and universities across the country. His work has appeared in various textbooks and anthologies including 'The National Geographic Book of Animal Poetry' edited by former Children's Poet Laureate of the United States, J. Patrick Lewis. His first book, 'Can I Touch Your Hair? Poems of Race, Mistakes and Friendship', co-written with Irene Latham, will be released by Milbrook Press in Fall 2017. For more information please visit: www.charleswaterspoetry.com

Damien Clarkson
Damien Clarkson is the Founder of Vevolution and director of the creative agency Growing Box where he helps social change organisations tell their stories. In 2016 he co-created SWINE, a short film exposing the rise of antibiotic resistance in factory farms. He is a widely published writer whose work can be found on the Guardian and Huffington post. Damien created Vevolution because he believes veganism is a social justice movement changing the world; and deserves a festival dedicated to education and community.

Dianne Sylvan

Dianne Sylvan is the author of 'The Shadow World' series of urban fantasy novels as well as two books on Neo-pagan spirituality, 'The Circle Within: Creating a Wiccan Spiritual Tradition' and 'The Body Sacred'. She lives, writes, and bakes wicked vegan cupcakes in Austin, Texas.

Dominic Berry

Dominic Berry is an internationally award winning vegan performance poet and workshop facilitator who works with both children and adults. His awards include winning New York's infamous *Nuyorican Poetry Cafe Slam*, winning Manchester Literature Festival's *Superheroes of Slam and, as of 2016, five Arts Council England Grants for the Arts awards to tour his theatrical vegan verse across the UK.*

Emily Atkinson-Dalton

Emily Atkinson-Dalton is a 22-year-old woman from Bath. Since she was a child she has been writing poetry and short fiction, and has recently begun writing again after finishing university. She has been vegan since she was twelve, and often incorporates animal rights issues into her writing, as well as other issues important to her. She has recently had a poem about homelessness accepted for publication, which is due out in December 2016 in the anthology 'Moments of Inspiration'.

Gabriel Colnic

Gabriel Colnic was born in the Republic of Moldova in 1994. He moved to the UK when he was 18 to pursue a career in acting. While still in his training at drama school, he discovered a passion for words and started exploring and experimenting with different forms of poetry. Through his work he wants to inspire and motivate people to always ask questions and to never accept anything as a given.

Gunjan Bhatia
A happenstance writer and an abolitionist vegan, Gunjan is also an energy healer, a classically trained dancer, and an adopted mom to a dog named Yuki. Having spent her life in three different continents, she considers herself a global nomad and is currently based in Southern California.

Honey Morris
Honey lives with her husband Stu, on 2.5 acres in picturesque Western Australia. They're passionate about transforming their land into a safe haven for WA wildlife and also, rescuing farmed animals, especially chickens. Honey is the creator of Veggie Yum Yums, a friendly vegan Facebook page and, when she's not making a mess in the kitchen, she enjoys the simple things in life; spending time with her family and friends, exploring the beautiful WA coastline, cruelty-free crochet, reading and of course, writing.

Karl Drinkwater
Sometimes Karl Drinkwater writes about life and love; sometimes death and decay. He usually flips a coin in the morning, or checks the weather, and decides based on that. His aim is to tell a good story, regardless of genre. When he is not writing or editing he loves exercise, guitars, computer games, board games, the natural environment, animals, social justice and zombies. He's been vegan for around 25 years. www.karldrinkwater.uk.

Katherine von Cupcake
Kat von Cupcake spent her pre-retirement years working as a San Francisco police officer. During her eight years in the K9 Unit, she realised the extraordinary intelligence and capabilities that animals possess. Her appreciation for animals and desire for the space to expand her understanding and love for other species landed her in Southern Oregon. Now Kat bakes compassionate treats for humans, and tends to her herd of rescued critters.

Keith Lupton

Keith Lupton lives in Perth, Western Australia and became vegan in 2015. He was inspired by the "No WA Shark Cull" rallies in 2014 and has since become an activist for several causes, mostly for animal rights. He is single with a 19-year-old son and is vegan for the animals, for the planet, and for his health (and in that order). He began the transition to veganism in 2014 and now can't go back.

Lenny Irukandji Marignier

Lenny Irukandji Marignier was born in France but raised in Sydney, Australia and now resides in the UK. Lenny's commitment to animal rights and the preservation of the planet started almost two years ago, from the moment they became a vegan. Lenny works closely with London Vegan Actions, the group responsible for the 'Earthlings Experience'. A visual artist by trade, many of their paintings and poems deal with animal rights issues.

Linda Monahan

Linda Monahan is an ethical vegan, writer, poet, priestess and flower essence practitioner. Linda has spent a year-long apprenticeship with a shamanic elder in the Goddess tradition and has gained the ability to share ancient wisdom about aligning our lifestyles with the natural rhythms of the earth, connecting with loving deities and elementals to support our healing and life path, reclaiming our personal power as women, and much more. Her writing has been published in 2016 in an academic anthology titled *Mourning Animals*, edited by Margo DeMello. www.tinyaffirmations.com.

Marc McGowan

Marc lives with his son and wife Valerie who is a social justice and vegan activist. Marc is an abolitionist, extreme blogger, movie-goer, gamer, comic, oversized teenager and critic of everything which can be critiqued. He loves his wife and children and even sees them every day. Marc and his wife are looking for new ways to advance the cause of peace, compassion and social justice for all.

M "Butterflies" Katz

M "Butterflies" Katz is an unwavering vegan of 37 years. (Vegetarian for nine years prior to that, starting at age 12 when her brother told her 'meat' was a dead animal and a cow's tongue was being served for dinner.) She is a (volunteer) vegan activist, author, writer, publisher, and pioneer. She is the editor of the book 'Why I will ALWAYS be vegan; 125 Essays from Around the World' and the author of the blog, 'Veganism; A Truth Whose Time has Come'.

Mango Wodzak

Mango Wodzak lives in the Australian tropics with his life partner Kveta. He has been vegan since the 1980s, and has written two books on the subjects of veganism and something he has christened *Eden Fruitarianism*, which he describes as an extension of the philosophy of veganism, embracing the ethics of respect, kindness and compassion for all life on earth, and understanding of mankind's true spiritual nature and physiological requirements. www.fruitnut.net.

Nancy Correa

The poetry and artwork Nancy Correa creates are a synthesis of 30 years as a vegan nonhuman/human animal rights activist. She has borne witness to and documented the atrocities considered standard practice in the flesh, hens' egg and animal milk agriculture industries as well as participated in hunt sabotages and other forms of direct action. The nonhuman animals have taught Nancy myriad lessons in compassion. She wants to impart those lessons through art and activism- artivism.

Nathan Hicks

Nate Hicks is an artist, musician, and writer with a burning desire to make people think. He has only been a vegan for two years, but does all he can to promote a healthy mind-set toward nutrition, animals, and our place on the Earth. He loves cooking, being outside, and enjoys almost every extreme sport. Nate lives in Burlington, Vermont and currently works as a Digital Designer.

Nicola Alexandra Evans
Nicola Alexandra Evans is a photographer and writer living in a quiet corner of the UK with her husband and son. She loves cooking and especially baking vegan treats for her family to enjoy.

Nicola McLean
Nicola McLean is an Irish artist living in Scotland's far north, with her paintings often influenced by her love of animals. She became vegetarian in 2011 following a throwaway comment on whether it was hypocritical to care for some animals while eating others. Nicola went vegan six months later after discovering the truth about dairy and egg farming and her only regret is not knowing enough to do it years earlier.

Philip Kiernan
Philip Kiernan is a vegan writer and artist living in Ireland. His work aims to highlight the suffering of animals around the world and inspire people to choose a compassionate path through life.

Philip McCulloch-Downs
Philip McCulloch-Downs has been creating art in various forms for all his life. He trained as an illustrator at Leicester Polytechnic, and then moved to Somerset in the UK in 2002 where he still lives. He became vegan upon joining Bristol-based charity Viva! (www.viva.org.uk) in 2003, and has been employed, educated and inspired by this organisation from that time onwards. Since 2014, he has been acknowledged as an Animal Rights Artist, and his paintings, poetry, novels and videos now have strong vegan/ethical themes. www.youtube.com/user/sbl2323.

Rekha Padinjattakathu
Rekha Padinjattakathu is a voracious reader and an avid traveler. She is passionate about nature and wildlife and loves spending time out in the wilderness. She enjoys exploring new possibilities and is currently pursuing a second Master's in Germany, where she resides with her husband and two little boys. Her work has been published and is forthcoming in several online publications like eFiction India, The Weekly Avocet, Hall of Poets etc. Rekha blogs in English and Malayalam @ wherethemindisforeverfree.wordpress.com

Robbie Nuwanda
Robbie Nuwanda is a lifelong vegetarian and now longstanding vegan. He is creative in a number of mediums, preliminary as an artist of impressionist painting but he also writes poetry and plays. In each medium he tries to promote veganism in a thought provoking and engaging way.

Robin Raven
Robin Raven is an author and journalist. Her debut children's book, "Santa's First Vegan Christmas", was published in June 2016. She holds a BFA from the School of Visual Arts and is now furthering her education. Robin blogs at RobinRaven.com and loves to connect with readers on social media. She often has her feet on a dance floor or her nose in a book, and delicious vegan food rocks her world.

Sea Sharp
Sea Sharp is a Pushcart Prize winner (2017), a Hammer and Tongue poetry slam finalist (Brighton, 2015/16), and a Prairie Seed Poetry Prize winner (2015/16). Sharp was the first featured poet on the Black Vegans Rock website (launched in 2016) and their debut book "The Swagger of Dorothy Gale & Other Filthy Ways to Strut" (Ice Cube Press) will be available on www.seathepoet.com; coming late Autumn 2016. Please follow @SeaThePoet .

Sky Raven the Vegan Poet
Sky Raven the Vegan Poet, was born, Abioseh Joseph Cole. He adopted his new name after going through a rite of passage with the indigenous Tsa-la-gi Choctaw Inter Tribal Nation, and being given the native name, Sky Raven. He began writing poetry in 1989 and is currently working on the completion of a collection of poems, 'Voices Unheard', geared specifically towards various disenfranchised social justice movements.

Susan Buckland
Susan Buckland lives in Melbourne, Australia. She has been vegan for over 24 years and feels fitter and healthier now than she did 24 years ago! Susan is a committed animal activist and dreams of the day when the whole world is vegan. Her motto is "Nothing tastes as good as being cruelty-free feels".

Susan Richardson
Susan Richardson is a poet, performer and educator whose third collection of poetry, 'skindancing', was published by Cinnamon Press in 2015. Susan is currently poet-in-residence with both the Marine Conservation Society, writing poems and running workshops in response to their 'Thirty Threatened Species' project, and the global animal welfare initiative, World Animal Day. She is the co-founder and poetry editor of *Zoomorphic*, the online literary journal that publishes writing in celebration and defence of animals. www.susanrichardsonwriter.co.uk

EMMA LETESSIER is a qualified PR professional and journalist, who also happens to be a passionate Christian vegan, animal and nature lover. She is the founder and editor of Barefoot Vegan Magazine (www.BarefootVegan.com), a bi-monthly digital magazine and website that empowers people to live their happiest and healthiest lives through working with nature. Barefoot Vegan is unique to many other vegan publications as not only does it provide information on health, diet and animal protection, it also promotes spiritual principles and alternative health practices, social justice and societal change, in addition to practical information regarding permaculture, environmental sustainability and self-sufficiency. It's also the official publication of the Barefoot Vegan Farm & Animal Sanctuary. All profits raised from the magazine go directly to the farm sanctuary. Emma grew up in New Zealand and moved to the United Kingdom at the age of 21. After 10 years in England, she now lives in the South West of France with her husband, Christian, and their dog, Hatchi on the farm that will soon become the Barefoot Vegan Farm and Animal Sanctuary (www.BarefootVeganFarm.com).

Photograph of Emma & Hatchi: Christian Letessier

Lightning Source UK Ltd.
Milton Keynes UK
UKHW022020281119
354410UK00013B/308/P